PRAYER

WRITTEN by Karen Dixon Merrell

ARTWORK by Dick Brown, Gary Kapp, Bob Reese

LITTLE DESERET STORIES ®

ISBN 0-87747-562-8

We talk to many people.

To our mothers and fathers —

To our brothers and sisters.

And to our friends
and neighbors.

Sometimes we even talk on the telephone to people we cannot see.

We thank people for helping us.

We ask people for things
that we need.

And we tell them about things that make us happy.

We can also talk to our
Heavenly Father.

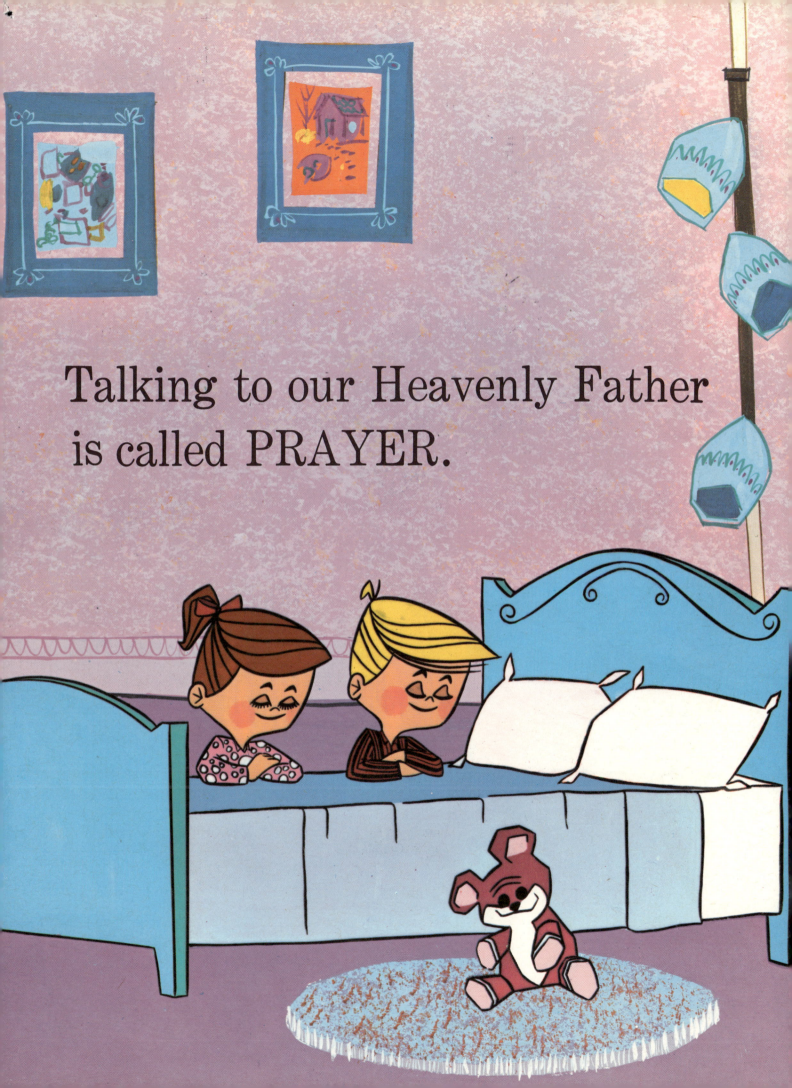

Talking to our Heavenly Father
is called PRAYER.

We can thank him for all our blessings.

Sometimes we need our Heavenly Father's help so we ask him in our prayers for what we need.

We can also tell him about things which make us happy.

When we talk to people we call them by their names, and when we pray we should begin by using our

HEAVENLY FATHER'S

name.

We can pray with our family every day. This is called family prayer.

Each day we also pray by ourselves. Our mother or father may need to help us at first but later we will be able to do it by ourselves.

Somebody prays for us in church.

There are special blessings
for new babies.

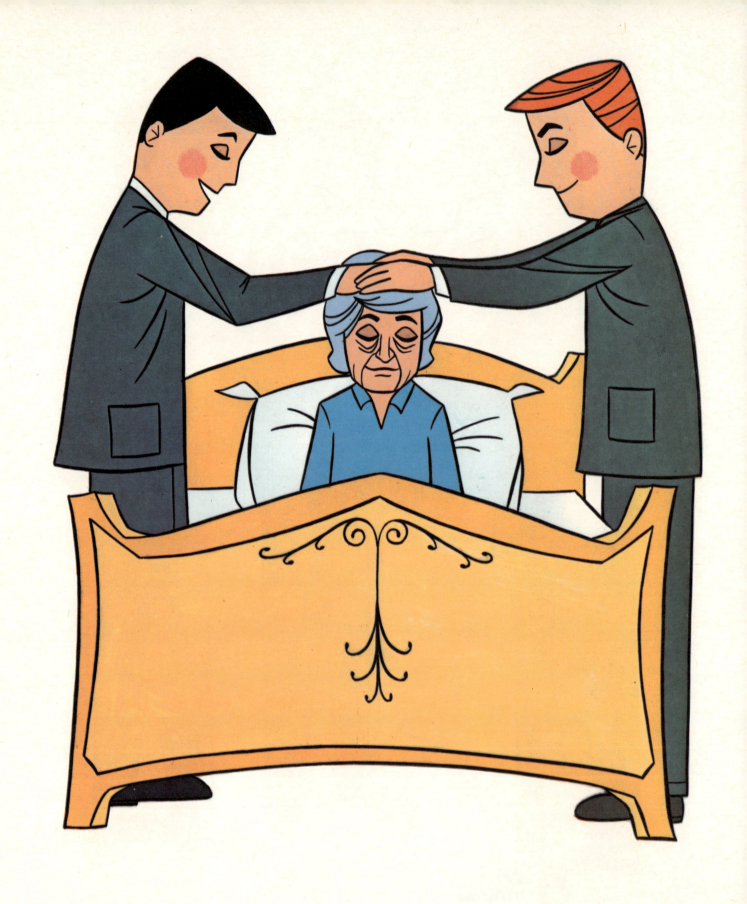

Someone who is sick

And those who have
just been baptized.

We also ask a blessing on the food.

All prayers should end in the name of

JESUS CHRIST

amen.